The Jubilee

Poems

by

John Blase

For Meredith

Contents

THE 12TH OF SEPTEMBER

ALMOST LIKE THE FIRST DAY OF SCHOOL

PROMISED

RESOLVE

FOR OUR OWN GOOD

AT SOME POINT ALONG THE WAY

WISHES

A DEFENSE OF MARRIAGE

AUTUMN AFFAIR

THE SKIN WE SPEAK

AS A FATHER I HAVE LEARNED

COMMON TRIBE

AS WE DROVE BACK

THE WAY HOME

CROSSING

THE COMING AND GOING

I DON'T BELIEVE I'VE EVER TOLD YOU

AS IT IS IN HEAVEN

THE CALLING IN WHAT REMAINS OF YOUR LIFE

THE NEXT DAY

REQUISITE

"We pray for salvation…when deliverance is so close at hand."

~ Harry Middleton, *The Bright Country*

THE BRAVEST THING

maybe the bravest thing
is opening your eyes in the
morning and placing your
two feet on the cold floor and
rising up against the gravity
of the night. maybe that's the
brave thing from which all other
bravery flows, the brave to
seek ye first. maybe that's the
single thing God requires of you,
the spiritual discipline that takes
all your will to muster. Swallow
down the fear, my friend, and face
the dawning day for what the
surface of the world needs most
of all is bravery skipping and
you, yes you are the stone.

I WANT TO LIVE IN A WORLD

I want to live in a world not prettified
but beautiful, the one that is actually here,
tart as wintergreen and rough as granite.

I want to live in a world of cashmere
and cleavage coupled with lonely churches beside
old cemeteries overgrown with moss.

I can't breathe in the world of red bows,
the one where truth is thin and castrated, where
God's mercies are always sweet and swift.

I want to die in a world where it rains,
where when the sky clears there are always ribbons.
God's justice can be slow, but it's sure.

THE WORLD'S CURVES

The poet notices
the world's curves.
The anti-poet is blind
to all but lines
missing out on
carousels at county fairs
and the roll of a foolish trout,
eyeless to a
woman's hips at dawn
and the tracks snaking beneath
God's wobbly train of justice.

THE CALL

One of the seraphim flew to me
with a live coal in each hand and
laid them upon my eyes.
And I saw the great deception was not
that we could be like God
but that we were bred solely for utility.
Then a voice gentle as rain said,
"Now go, tell them they were born
to be monumental in the sun."

IT IS NOT SO MUCH

Its not so much that I do not do the good
that I want to do as it is I sometimes do not
do simply because I am unsure what to do.
Some would label this passivity, the same
some who hold assertiveness as a virtue
although for the life of me I cannot find
that in any sacred text save the american bible.

This same some (apparently) forge through life
with a plan, a map they chart by bolder stars.
I on the other hand wake to mild confusion most
days not about the tiny aspects of self-respect
such as brushing my teeth and paying my bills
but more the big things like my destiny, etc.

Oh this mobile home of flesh that is me!
Who or what will rescue me from me?

Thanks be to God that best I can tell my calling
is to life, the specifics of which have a tendency
(so far) to work themselves out. So I press on
honestly trying to do the next thing in love.
And while that does sound poetic it at the same

time I must confess sounds awfully flimsy when presenting myself to those who swear to have the world on a string, this life by the tail.

THE HIGHER COST OF LOVING

Most nights Jesus rubs his wrists after the world
has laid itself down to sleep.
And there they are – the scars.
As on earth, so still in heaven.
Time's passing has not obscured them nor the
memory of their occurrence.

Some nights the remembrance is dull, almost sour.
But most are vivid, when to place his finger on
the rind of pain is to be suddenly and at once back
there as nails and men did what they did.
True, they had no idea. But they knew.

Upon his return the scars created an impedance in
heaven, a resistance to how things had been.
God was clear: This is my son, I am sore pleased.
But Christ's wounds keep him forever alien, not fully
home, not fully prodigal. He reigns
pulled in two directions, between thieves.

WHAT SUCH A CLAIM MIGHT AT LAST ENTAIL

His was a gentleness of necessity. Not what he
should or ought to do. But what he must.
Christ lived as a man might live only near the end
of his life, in a way that militates against putting
off what one has to do. In his awful incongruity
he was love perishing, pure gentleness in memory
and melody, Christmas in the wilderness.
That's what made men drop their lives and follow.

WHAT THE BELOVED HEARD

Most commentators insist that
when the beloved disciple leaned
back into Jesus' bosom he heard
the heartbeat of God. Or possibly
the pulse of compassion. Or something
similarly soothing to our senses.
This is yet another example of the
mistake the commentator mind makes,
trying to think beyond what it knows.
John's proximity gave him access to
Christ's longing. And anyone who knows
knows that meant he was near enough
to hear the universal whisper that
revealed Jesus truly was our brother:
I just want to make my old man proud.

ELEGY AND PSALM

He was ramshackle,
one of three thieves
bleeding out like a stuck pig.
To see it was to witness
an immodest poem.
No one knew exactly
what it meant but we all knew
how it made us feel –
fleeced.
His last words are recorded.
There were others though,
not written down but entrusted
to our hands. We carried
them like a birthright
from that moment on. I recall
he looked at me and said,
"Now nothing in this world
is plain, John. Nothing."

THE MAGDALENE

She loved him because
his ways were gentle.
How he came to be like
that she did not know
and did not care.
It was enough that he was.
He always greeted her
the way morning breaks,
sharp but soft.
He did not come to rescue her
as most men defined rescue:
to bend and to douse.
He came lighting the way
for her to stand and burn.

VARIATION ON THE PRODIGAL

Years after the break that broke
our father's heart, he came back.
He hadn't come to his senses as
much as he'd grown deathly sick,
some wasting disease contracted
in the country far away from us.

I'd buried our father in those saddest
years, dug his grave all by myself.
The servants were let go by then.
I'd also buried my wife and our son.
Only the wind and ghosts remained.

He said I didn't know where else to go.
I said Its right that you came home.
So we attempted to bridge the time
though we were older men by then.
We hoped to find ourselves again as
boys who were also once brothers.

I cared for him like he prayed I would.
He wondered whether this was out of
duty or due to love. I said I cannot say.

Such categories lose their meaning after
so much is lost and poorly grieved.
I told him I'm glad you came home.

When he died I wrapped him in our
father's faded robe and buried him by
the others out back beneath the oaks.
I left the next day with my inheritance
of memories and our father's signet ring.
I saw tomorrow from still a long way off.

PSALM FAINTLY

Oh, LORD, today is already too much.
A part of me says grief, don't be such a drama king

while another part of me says there, there, pal,
it'll all be okay, just do your best, alright?

Then there is that other part of me, saner than the
rest, holding the negatives of your mercies

up to the coming light seeing darkly what has been.
The past is my only ground of hope. That you

were faintly there, as you feel now, will have to be
enough on this day that already feels too much.

PART, BUT NOT ALL

There are days appointed
for you to suffer. On these days
you must simply endure.
There is no silver lining.
Only the bitter of dust.
Don't pray to the Twitter-god
on such days. His 140-character
belchings mock the very dignity
that is your life.
Find a crucifix instead, if only one
cobbled in your throbbing head,
one that conjures up the profanity
of that godforsaken thirty-something
holding on for his dear life.
Then look up, if you dare, up into
the bottomless playground of birds
and listen close to their hilarity.
The suffering is part, but not all.

AND THE GREATEST OF THESE

Until your tears have fermented
they are only water,
easily mistaken for raindrops.
But should you endure the season
your grief might turn to wine,
your sadness might become
the spirit others will travel
far and wide to taste.
Know that the season is often long,
the weather harsh and inappropriate.
There are no guarantees.
Only hope, wait, and see remain.
And the greatest of these is hope.

TURN, TURN

There comes a time to commit
yourself to the scripture of matter.
A season to seek second
the words of God and become first
a disciple of his handiwork.
A time to study the historical context
of aunts and uncles. A time to translate
your dreams paying close attention
to correct tense. A time to read
the evening skies from right to left.
Hide all these turnings deep within
yourself so that as time flies and days
pass you might not sin in vain.

TO THINK I THOUGHT

There were those
born into a house of prose:

    Wash those dishes.

    Take out that trash.

    Don't you sass me.

But I was
born into a house of poetry:

    Shiloh, when I was young…

    He maketh me to lie down in green pastures…

    Baby sister, I was born game…

And to think I thought
we once were poor.
Now I remember different.

BOUND AWAY

I often walk beside a creek with no name
bursting with frog song. They're singing
"Shenandoah." Or at least that's what I hear.
As I walk I dream dreams of my father
and the love I feel for that unsung man
reaches inside my chest and turns my
aging heart one notch counterclockwise.
It is on those walks as the dark gathers
close to the ground to envelop me that I
find, as the Quakers say, peace at the center.

ABSOLUTE SWAY

He sits with his mother in room 710.
The pain from her broken back is not
quite so proud today so they seize the
chance to talk because they both know
time is thinning. Her memory at 88 is
still hungry so he lures her to the waters
of that old hymn – "Have Thine Own Way."
She follows for her sake as much as his.
With dulcet voice she sings a song sung
many times over but now the notes work
toward her final molt so she can rise to fly.
He sits in her waiting, yielded and still.

THIS IS WHAT WE DO

His sole brother will be another year older this week.
So my father will drive headlong into the north Texas
wind to sit across from him and honor his face.

No doubt they will speak of pickups and children
until those topics grow quiet. Then their talk will seep
into the porous ground of memory recent and past.

Two older men talking fondly of older things,
the essence of why they want to be together.
Before my father leaves that booming town he'll

wind beyond the frantic to the still cemetery where
his parents sleep. He will go there repeating Easter's
mistake, seeking the living among the dead.

My father knows this, but still he'll go. To kneel and
to place fresh flowers, an assertion in favor
of the rising, and against the fallenness of time.

MY FATHER'S COFFEE

My father's coffee is instant.
Boil some water, add the crystals,
stir, and there you have it.
For years now I have been the
imperialist prodigal
returning to my father's house with
my own wife and children, and coffee.
I imported Costa Rica Peaberry and
Major Dickason's and once some
chickory blend dark as
the inside of a whale.
My father would yield each time,
making allowances for my
far countrying due to his great love.
I would leave and he would
find again his Folger's, like water
returning to a low spot.
I may have broadened his horizon
but I never changed his mind.
But now, with him at his age
and me at mine, I would much
rather be his son than sophisticated.
So from now until then,

when in my father's house
I will drink as my father drinks.
In his house there is instant coffee.
If it were not so, I would have told you.

THE 12TH OF SEPTEMBER

This is the day the Lord hath made.
This is also the day Cash died.
So while I find joy in the making I also
shoulder grief at the taking of one whose
voice was second only to my father's
when I was a boy and growing.
And sometimes, when my father would
lose himself and sing of unbroken circles,
those two voices, they were one.

ALMOST LIKE THE FIRST DAY OF SCHOOL

She held me longer than usual this time
as we said our goodbyes.
She rubbed the clay of my back, sculpting
my shape in the space before her so
she could stand in that kitchen after I drove away
and remember clearly what she once made.
We both cried. Hers were familiar tears,
those of parting. She is my good mother.
Mine flowed from fears that I may have
lived a careless life. I am her oldest son who
lives now beyond the edge of the drive.

PROMISED

To last the winter requires
desire. Your ancestors knew this.
They sailed in wagons from Tennessee
to the New World (Texas),
settling there in a crevice of
mediocrity, their vision daily
whipped by an ever chilling wind.
They look on you now calm-eyed
from the fair banks of Canaan,
your own cloud-burst of witnesses.
They claim you. But they're worried
about your core: you're wobbly.
You've put too much stock in who's
following rather than where you're bound.
Your ancestors knew above all else
you must have a center.
The winter can be long.

RESOLVE

What do you do when you discover
your inheritance is too small for you,
that all your instruction and training
were intended to create the guts for
you to say, "I'm leaving now, goodbye."
The far country doesn't have to be a
place of wasting. It can be a horizon
of spending yourself in extravagant
gestures never dreamed of by your
father and his fathers before him.
You must not look your father in his
eyes as you walk away. He knows you are
his son but you are also the offspring of
wild, rangy, boom-bust ancestors who
would not suffer fences. He knows there
will be no tableau of homecoming,
yet his shoulders rise with sorrow's pride.

FOR OUR OWN GOOD

Time passes so quickly we forget
the extravagance of loss until something plain
stands in our way to say: Remember.
Opening the refrigerator to see a jar of olives
that treat your father loved to snack on.
Standing in the checkout line as
the overhead speaker plays "Love Is Blue"
that tune your mother swayed to
as she did the dishes at night.
Such somethings find their way into our
distracted days for our own good,
so we might not forget what we mean – to be loving.

AT SOME POINT ALONG THE WAY
time begins to hemorrhage.
Efforts to slow its flow are vain.
Go ahead and try so you can say
I tried. But I'll say I told you so.
Whatever you thought life close
to fifty would look like, it doesn't.
You find yourself sifting among
the ruins searching for clues as to
what you've been doing all these years.
You come across a pill-box full of
children's teeth, a half-read copy
of *Blood Meridian*, fading obituaries
of classmates, and the black seeds of
dreams planted that you still have
hope might one day soon bloom.

WISHES

Be careful what you wish for.
If you wish to be a man's man
you might find yourself at the end
a hard-pressed man who missed
the daily frailties that soften you
allowing you to close your eyes
and rest in peace. Perhaps the
grander wish is to be a woman's man
or a child's man or a dog's man.
Those are the men missed when
they are finally gone.

A DEFENSE OF MARRIAGE

Marriage is the doorway to the second half
of the world, one long learning of what you can't
do for another person, a shared wrap of yesterdays
woven with small expressions of disappointment yet
each one dyed deep by the hitchhiker's joy that
someone on the great lonely road stopped to say,
"Why don't you and I go together?" Such happiness
often begins on cicada-laden afternoons in the time
of the year the Sioux call The Moon of Making Fat.

AUTUMN AFFAIR

We really didn't have the time.
Then again we've been together
long enough to know time is no
commodity but a fire in which we
suffer loss and are purged.
So we left the children to themselves
and drove higher up the mountain,
higher than we live, up where the
aspens were already arrogant.
You took my hand and we walked
Preacher's Hollow trail, you making
jokes about hollow preacher heads.
We laughed quiet so as not to douse
the falling embers on our shoulders.
I pocketed one of those leaves to press
in the Stegner novel we both love.
Maybe one day our children will open
that book and the leafy memory of
their parents' autumn affair will fall
to the floor and they will understand
we really didn't have the time.

THE SKIN WE SPEAK

Words are skin pulled tight
over the meat of our intent.
To speak the words I'm sorry
is epidermal etiquette beneath
which lies bloody raw sadness
striated with regret.
To offer this without words would
only further repel the heart of
one you love, so you say I'm sorry.
And you hope your skin is thin
enough the transgressed can
see below and forgive.

AS A FATHER I HAVE LEARNED

We were taught that if God made us
strong then weakness is a blasphemy.
All I can say is that'll carry you for a
decade, maybe, if you're lucky, then
you'll be tempted to lose character.
For example, you'll start eating donuts
with a fork or folding your boxer shorts.
If you hope to make it as a father you'd
best learn to stand alone in the yard
at night and allow your human failings
of the day to be absorbed by the stars.
I say this not in theory but as practitioner.
No one taught me this. I stumbled upon
the discipline in a used book about myths.
No matter how much you want to take
the pain away from those closest to you
the vital truth is you cannot. This will
almost always feel like trespass. But you've
done nothing wrong except to love them.

COMMON TRIBE

I once read that as bitter March winds
blew Crazy Horse cradled his daughter's
still body in his arms and lay down with
her on a small burial platform as she died
from the white man's cough. She was called
They Are Afraid of Her, his only daughter.
As this greatest of all Sioux men held her
tightly in a red blanket the wolves sang a
beautiful chorus and she was lifted into a
better heaven than our own. I am not a
Sioux chief but I am a father so I believe
he tried to summon her back to life as Jesus
did to Lazarus, but found he could not.
I read further that ravens black as pitch
began to circle overhead the lifeless red
bundle as Crazy Horse rode away hard
with tears loosened by the cold wind that
blew the colder stars around the sky.
Then, as a father, I became so lost in my
own visions I simply could read no more.

AS WE DROVE BACK

As we drove back home from the Rock House
the day was ending and the small town where
we live hummed quietly. In the backseat my little
girl finished her ice cream cone and talked with her
mother about a movie they both can't wait to see.
As they spoke I drove slower than the limit, tucking
the scenes in my mind – the fire station's faithful
watch, the meadow where the quarter horses play,
the geraniums in front of the Presbyterian church,
the lights of the prosperous east side, and the geese.
I wondered if my daughter will return some day to
gain an older sense of this place where she became,
if she might buy a cone for her little girl, then drive
around slow showing her the pieces of our dream.

THE WAY HOME

Why I still save paper receipts I do not know
other than they are pages from our book of living.
I bought fourteen gallons of mid-grade gas Monday

so we could drive to Denver to enjoy hamburgers
and then shop for ripped-up blue jeans. All of this
stored in my memory banks but should something go

horribly haywire so I missed my trains of thoughts
these black and white slips serve as fragile
cairns so presumably a man could find his way home.

CROSSING

Across the simple meadow of my heart
stands an aging barn, older but sure,
painted red not fire engine but red
more decadent, like blood.
For years I've stacked my secrets
there in the loft like hay, happy now
to pitch them down to rupture and spill
so you can better understand
the choir of flesh I am.
I will do this, gladly. But first you must
cross the simple meadow of my heart.

THE COMING AND GOING

A deep-yellow dove more
brilliant than gold came to
me to die. I said See I'm not
a doctor, and she said I know
but you look at the world and
into your heart at the same time.

So I spent her last day listening
to her sing of this world, what
she called the Suchness. I held
her in my fragile hands and felt
the shape of death. I held her to
the very end and then a little more.

I DON'T BELIEVE I'VE EVER TOLD YOU

Are you ever afraid of dying?
I'm not talking about
the dying that will deposit you
directly into the Lord's presence (as some hold).
But the dying that will tear
you from the fabric of here,
here where you've seen wonders.
I don't believe I've ever told you I fear
that second kind of dying. But I do.
I'm telling you now because I've recently
seen how life changes in an ordinary instant,
reminds us we live in a game of gossip,
whispering our stories to the next in line.
We die. Then we're passed along in
another's tongue, and I'm afraid they'll
edit a crucial detail.

AS IT IS IN HEAVEN

I'd like to believe we die and are reborn in heaven
as infants who will learn everything once again.
God will be the father and mother we always wished
for,
the parent who will hold our hand and walk slow
with us in the evening and say,
"Listen, do you hear that? That is the whippoorwill."
and
"Look, look up there. That is the moon."
The first time we reach for the rose's stem
we'll find the thorn and draw back in pain.
God will take our palm and say,
"Now that is a thorn. And this is your blood."
God will smile and smear the crimson tear away
with spit and then we will continue on.

THE CALLING IN WHAT REMAINS OF YOUR LIFE

The eyes of the aspen are watching to see
if before you cross over to that next place
you'll take your simple life and grind it up
in your imagination so as to build exquisite
arbors of memory your children and children's
children can stand beneath and find shade.
If you are faithful to this calling then future
generations might pause beneath the shelter
of your effort, shored up with the knowing
that one of their kin dared each day to look
unafraid into the very heart of this sorrowed
heaven on earth and that even in the vex of
grief said thank you, thank you for it all.
The eyes of the aspen are watching to see
if you'll spend the remains of your life this way.
If so these earthly angels promise gold as you
surrender, a quaking whisper of those
forgotten words from the old book: well done.

THE NEXT DAY

There are times as a writer when
you must practice forbearance.
Some evenings the pall of death

is so heavy halfway around the world
that you search for paper and pen
to try and make your sense of it.

Better to go mow the emerald grass
in diagonal rows and pull purple thistles
from the fence and startle the grey rabbit

beneath the shade tree and speak to your
very much alive neighbors as they walk by
while the summer wind chills the sweat inching

down your back and for reasons unknown
you suddenly recall the sinful smell of your
grandfather's tobacco mingled with the

memory of the tears in your wife's eyes
as the doctor placed your firstborn son in the
crook of her arm and life demanded on.

REQUISITE

You may turn away
from the complexity that is
your life. But then you must live
with the consequences
of turning away.
We wish upon some static star
to bring order to our days.
We forget stars shine only by
burning, flames the
requisite for grace.

PRIVILEGE OF EXILES

Nine, no make that ten

blackbirds in the

top of the stark white Aspen tree

each on his own branch in

stair

   step

      fashion

like something from the mind

of Annie Dillard (the early years).

Suddenly the ten burst black

pressing hard into

the ever beguiling western sky.

Did the wind

or their kin

alert them to some change, some wickedness coming?

Or did the ten agree

to linger in a tree

just long enough so a man might bear

witness to our privilege,

we exiles upon

this radiant spinning plane?

GOOD COMPANY

There is something everlasting
in those classic westerns
when the cowboy kisses the
lady near the bend in the river
where the cottonwoods grow.
For that scene she reins in her
power to make room for him,
so he can taste the ambrosial
wind on her mouth and feel
the pulse of the whole world.
In that kiss he realizes she is
good company to keep, that
by her side he might transcend
the genre's fence to grow into
a man who loved too much.

THEIR SIDES TOUCHING

Suddenly quiet that winter's afternoon
she asked if he'd ever heard the bells at
the end of Copland's "Appalachian Springs."
He said no, for he never had.
So she led him by the hand to sit in front
of her father's console where they leaned
in close, touching, listening all the way
to the untroubled end, there were the
bells chimed three times so tender.
Her hair smelled of cinnamon and he was felled by
something he could not pronounce as a
boy but remembers now as a man this winter's day.

THINGS BELOW

Instead of struggling to not be conformed to this world, why not practice further prying open the breastbone of our fragile existence, reaching deeper into creation's core to seize more and more of the pulsing fist of life?

Instead of straining to stay unspotted from this world, why not say I do to flesh and blood, and commit yourself to a people and a place, and vow to love and be loved in return?

It's a hard business being human.

It's much easier to hover above your days as some wispy holier-than-the-rest-of-us. But even if your job performance is mediocre, the consolation for trying is you'll end up with memories instead of regrets.

Leave cleverness to the angels. Set your mind on things below.

THE BEAUTIFUL NEVER GO FAR

It often takes a death
to create the noble sense
to stand still, to listen and observe
the glad and fearful story.
And so you do, you stop
and notice the day is clear as gin
and you're alive not because
you've been living right
(you know better than that)
but rather because you're alive.
And so you vow to write
more letters, to try to have some
style even if you fail, and to care about
something well done.
And so you stand on that ginny day
in your uninnocent feet with
a green wind out of the north,
miles away from an old friend's grave
worrying and worrying the hope that,
as *the poet put it:
the beautiful never go far.

*Richard Hugo

ACTUALLY, SCRATCH THAT

The timeline's different for each of us
but at some point you have to stop fighting
your parents or religion or 1950s America or
your no-good-cheating-ex-spouse
or quite possibly even yourself. Yes, yourself.
Signify this truce by beating your sword
into a plowshare. Actually, scratch that.
I propose beating it into wind chimes.
That way you'll be gently recalled to the
forgiveness when subsequent winds blow.
Those notes will be a charmer's tune
easing the air around you, an alarming
remembrance that by no means did you give up,
but that by choice you gave in to an older song.

AN OLDER WOMAN

1.

Hers is a used and casual
beauty, the best kind actually for
it never needs to trumpet itself.
It simply is, like the world.

2.

She's lived by rising and falling,
perfecting symphonies of self-love.
Her speech is worn smooth as the
throats of wild flowers.

3.

She thinks with her body
which means she thinks long,
lithe, limber thoughts.
But she can't stand missionaries.

4.

Her dreams are as dark as
last night's wine, which is to
say she sleeps sound and sane,
with untroubled eyes.

5.

She believes in a grounded heaven –

people will still have sex,

and we'll keep our four seasons.

But she predicts pedicures for free.

LOVE IN THE TIME OF PARANOIA

If love is for real
and not just a word
then show me.
I know you're frightened.
I am too.
But that is the feeling
imperfect people
always have as they
row closer home.

FORGIVE US

We've no clue how adored we are, tiptoeing
through this knotted green world on egg shells
with our fists clenched tight rehearsing our
litanies of trouble all the while rationing breaths
afraid of running out of misery.
We royals eking out an existence based on scarcity
when the truth is the banquet is spread before us.
Teach us to fall against the earth. Train us to
listen for the wind's chamber music.
Warn us the world is so necessary.

(lagniappe – "a little something extra")

JUBILEE

This is my body
bones brittler than
a decade ago
eyes dependent
to glass distances
middle thickening
against my pleas
mind content to
mine yesterdays.
But my heart still
breaks then mends
breaks then mends
like always.

Acknowledgments

Mom and Dad, thanks for your excitement about this collection. And thanks, Mom, for helping me whittle the number down to fifty. That you took such an interest in helping me choose what would be included here humbled me. And that you said, "But the final choices are yours, John," well, that broke me.

Shawn, I couldn't have managed the cover design without you. That your eyes and hands are a part of this makes me happier than you know. Mucho thanks, brother.

Winn Collier, your belief in and advocacy of this wacky idea has kept me on the rails. To have a friend like you is nothing less than a gift. I mean that.

Meredith, I'm not sure if this is my side hustle or my side shuffle. You know how horribly slow I move. But you kept encouraging and encouraging. I love you, kiddo.

Will, Sarah, and Abbey, your faces and laughter haunt these pages, every one of them.

And goodness, Lord, not a lick of this would even be possible if not for your infinitely tender hand. As Jimmy Dean sings, "I'm drinking from my saucer, 'cause my cup has overflowed." Goodness, Lord. Thanks.

31399749R00039

Made in the USA
Columbia, SC
02 November 2018